Her Addiction

An Empty Place at the Table

poems by

Mary Sexson

Finishing Line Press
Georgetown, Kentucky

Her Addiction

An Empty Place at the Table

Copyright © 2023 by Mary Sexson
ISBN 979-8-88838-271-4 First Edition
All rights reserved under International and Pan-American Copyright Conventions. No part of this book may be reproduced in any manner whatsoever without written permission from the publisher, except in the case of brief quotations embodied in critical articles and reviews.

Publisher: Leah Huete de Maines

Editor: Christen Kincaid

Cover Art: Courtesy of Paul Young Photography

Author Photo: Susie Wagner

Cover Design: Elizabeth Maines McCleavy

Order online: www.finishinglinepress.com
also available on amazon.com

Author inquiries and mail orders:
Finishing Line Press
P. O. Box 1626
Georgetown, Kentucky 40324
U. S. A.

Table of Contents

The Token 1
Here Beside Him 2
Only Memories to Guide You 3
Color of My Heart 4
Vodka Memories 5
The Hatch Blown 6
The Sense of You 7
Getting Sober 8
On Our Knees 9
The Pain in You 10
You, On Crack 11
Sleep the Sleep 12
Your Father and I 13
Insomnia 14
Sadder People 15
String of Days 16
Higher Ground 17
This, Over and Over 18
Second Baptism 19
The Space You Occupy 20
Grief Shapes Us 21
An Empty Place at the Table 22
Protocols 23
His Life Goes On 24
A Simple Gesture 25
Put Back the Stars 26
The Dinosaur Game 27
Tell Her 28

All the Whys 29

Growing Pain 30

Map of My Fears 31

Wrapped up in Normal 32

Recovery 33

Out of the Maze 34

Metaphorically Speaking 35

Back into the Fray 36

Big Ironman 37

Raising You 38

The Syntax of Your Texts 39

This Mother's Lament 40

In the Throes of Your Addiction 41

Paperwork 42

Driving Away from You 43

Recovery Redux 44

To the Universe, Clumsily 45

Clean 46

Disparity 47

In and Out 48

Recompense 49

Anything Can Happen 50

The Gut of Your Habit 51

Can You Spell R-E-L-A-P-S-E? 52

More Bigger Blues 53

Holding Our Breath 54

On Being Thrown Out of Rehab 55

Suicide, By Installments 56

Rewriting the Script 58

The Words 59

This book is dedicated to my daughter, Sarah, who is in recovery, working as an addictions therapist in a rehabilitation treatment center, and using her story to help other recovering addicts.

*Left to our own devices
like maybe they were too
out on the open road
and wondering what to do*

*You ask how we got here baby don't ask how
that was sometime other than now*

"Sometime Other Than Now"
Written By John Hiatt
Universal Careers Publishers

The Token

Your fragile world
balances itself
on a small precipice
of possibility. If you
can get through today
without a drink
tomorrow will come
with a feeling of forgiveness.
You will be able to tap
the keg of atonement
and look like you really mean it.

Your start-over token
is shiny in your pocket.
It holds the odds
of everything
you want, maybe even
your own redemption.
So much rides
on this thin metal coin,
a triangle of promise
etched with a prayer.

Here Beside Him

The World is spinning
in its orbit today.
There is not
a boy looking for his mother.

She is here beside him
reading the book
about dinosaurs
that he loves.

She colors with him
at the kitchen table,
she lays beside him
while they watch TV.

She fixes his lunch, helps him
with his shoes, chats with him
about dinosaur bones.
He tells her he is "scared of Santa"
and they talk quietly about it.

Today the boy is with his mother
and the world feels right.

Only Memories to Guide You

How will you find your way back
to the life you had? What will it take
to show you the way? There are only
memories to guide you, to help you
recognize the parts worth saving.

Tonight, I want to pretend everything
is fine. You never started drinking
again, you did not tell me to go fuck myself,
you did not cast your eyes down
in shame, unwilling and unable to meet mine.

You want to pretend there is nothing
worth staying sober for, or that you can stop
drinking whenever you like. We want
to pretend, together, that your boy
will be just fine. How will you find
your way back to the life you had?
There are only memories to guide you.
Will you recognize the parts worth saving?

Color of My Heart

The indigo sky, color of my heart
today, blue tattooed across it,

the ink that bleeds itself unwashable.
I try walking it off, letting my thoughts

merge with the cloudless horizon.

Sweat comes off me, a cleansing
of sorts, the salt bitter like a sacrament

on my skin. I promise not to speak
of this sadness, lest it color the night too.

Vodka Memories

The brush around the small pond
has grown up over the years
since I threw your vodka bottles
into the water there, trying to keep you
from getting arrested for a DWI.

Your brother and I cleaned up the evidence
before the tow truck got there to take
your car to a repair shop.
You'd been lucid enough
to call us, grateful, I believe,
that you'd lived, and not killed anyone
when you drove up out of that ditch
and slid across Binford Boulevard.

Maybe there really are spirits somewhere
who look after the incompetent,
keep them alive until their time comes.
However it works, you were protected
that night, made to live; maybe so you
could tell your story, years later,
to some other drunk who would be trying
to get sober for a reason, any reason at all.

The Hatch Blown

Your pain is palpable
and smeared across your face,

the smile slightly displaced,
your hands nervous

inside your pockets. The truth
of your unhappiness

is being revealed to you
even as I write this, the nut

is cracked, the hatch blown.
I could have told you

it would end this way, you
barely breathing while
the planet keeps spinning.

The Sense of You

It's good to have you back again.
I see the evenness in your step,
the cautious smile, your humor
trying itself on again. It's such a loss
when you give in to the alcohol,
such a heavy toll to pay, for all
of us.
                The sense of you now
is so vivid and defined, not the blur
of your drunken self, the one who lies
and cannot look me in the eye.

                I know your struggle.
I've witnessed the pain,
I've come face-to-face
with the ugliness of this addiction
and every time it leads me to this place,
on my knees imploring the universe
to release you from these bonds.

Getting Sober

We have taken you
to raise a second time,
hoping this one sticks.
We feel like our lives
depend on it.
                    You store your things
in the spare room, next
to the narrow bed of your youth.
We talk about house rules,
ask to meet friends
who pick you up for meetings.
We set the alarm to a new code,
take away your keys and drive you
to wherever else you need to go,
returning to the days
before you got your license,
you dependent and pissed off.
                    Your dad and I whisper
about whether this will work.
Will you stay clean
if we leave you alone
and unwatched? The price we all pay
for this level of intimacy is staggering.
We know each other's dreams
and fears, dark moments
exposed like reality TV.
                    Through it all
we can hear the moments tick by,
the cost of your sobriety counted
day by precious day,
marking off the time when
we're not so scared,
when we sit in our chairs and breathe.

On Our Knees

Your addiction has cut
into the heart of us, opened
a new vein and drawn blood,
knocked us to our knees
with no time for prayers.
You outplay us all,
a girl who can slink
down any alley looking for drugs
and live to talk about it,
a trophy story dark enough
to impress even
the toughest old-timers.

Now the truth checks in,
a half-way house,
your boy gone,
your accounts emptied,
and you at the sharpened edge
of real.

We settle
into an out-of-sync routine,
us with your boy,
you with the doctor,
not one of us at peace.
                The days unfold
like sympathy cards
that cannot hold
the weight of our sadness.

The Pain in You

The pain in you will not subside
with the margarita you made,
or be soothed by a pull
on the crack pipe.	This pain
that lives in your DNA cannot
be bought off with heroin or rum.
It exists on a primitive level,
the script written centuries ago
with the ink of fear and self-loathing,
a cocktail of grief downed
over and over again.	It subsists now
on a molecular level, in blood cells
and skin, woven into muscle and bone,
it moves as you move, breathes
as you breathe.

You, On Crack

I watched your spectacular fall
from the wings, not wanting to share
your stage, it belonged so completely
to you.

You, on crack, defies description.
I am silent as you slur your speech,
wipe the eyeliner off your cheek, beg
me to leave so I won't see you like this.

You, driving down Boulevard, crying,
calling your father to save you, somehow,
from this pathetic journey, screaming for him
to stop this car and get you out.

Now you're on the couch, cursing us, hating
what you have become and slamming
the sense of it around the room so we
can really feel it.

This is you, on crack, your real self
lost in the flush of this high you desire,
lost to us in the blur
of your halcyon days.

Sleep the Sleep

You blew the top off, darlin',
and shook our little world up

like it'd been hit by a bomb.
The crack, the jive, the lies,

all padded the bed you'd made
for yourself. Sleep the sleep

little one, lay down on that bed
of yours and feel the ache

seep into your bones, turn yourself
over when you can stand the light.

Your Father and I

With you tucked in now
to the half-way house,
there is really nothing left
to do but sit back and wait
to see if this cure will take.

Your father and I chat quietly
about how you seem each day.
We weigh the tone of your voice
with the pallor of your skin,
whether or not you jiggle
your leg as you sit and recount
your time at a meeting.

Did you mention how many days
you had? Did it seem sincere?
Can we go on the vacation we planned
a year ago, before you decided
you liked the way crack made you feel?

This tired wagon, its wheels
no longer sticking to the road,
its driver off course, us in back,
your truly captive audience.

Insomnia

At four-thirty in the morning
the world seems wide open,
not close enough to catch me
as I am falling through its cracks.

I wake up with thoughts of you
hunkered down tight in my right
frontal lobe, memories of our lives
skidding past in a quick-clip video.

I need to look at these pictures,
try to find out where it was I
screwed up, made the mistakes,
dropped the ball, erred humanly.

I cannot get a grip on rational
thinking, so I toss it all in,
toe the floor looking for my house shoes,
headed into full wakefulness.

Walking downstairs I see TV light
on the darkened living room walls.
Your father is awake too. We are both
mired in the ugly pit of doubt and worry.

We view the screen wordlessly, he scans
through infomercials and cooking shows.
We settle on a season finale we had missed,
lean back to sink our consciousness in.

It is over before we realize it, and I see
I have cried silently for the heroine's plight,
her inability to be with her lover, her sheer loss
of self. We rise together, then, seeking dawn.

Sadder People

The days
just keep coming,
no reprieve, no stopping
to reassess, ponder, rethink
the plan for living.

I look
for a corner to huddle in,
but instead I stay up late, eat
bad food, watch terrible
crime shows endlessly.

I want to know
somewhere else
there are worse things,
sadder people
than here.

String of Days

I will gladly stand here
at the open door to this
string of days, unwritten,
unspoken, undreamed,
and yet they are fully formed
in my head, plotted and schemed
for the better, the new deal,
the hope and desire I have
for the girl who lost her way.
She wanders the planet
alone now, untethered, her ballast
cut loose so she could fly.

But I will haul her back to earth,
moor her to this life, sit back
and watch her live it out
with all her charm and gusto.
She will not regret one moment,
not one second of this gravity.

Higher Ground

We've passed the middle point now,
where it would be safe to turn back.
We went so far beyond it we don't
even remember how it used to be
between us. I have a recollection
of how you looked and sounded,
but it is imprecise and clogged
with sodden pictures that tell another
story.
         You call and text relentlessly,
pleading your case
over and over again as if
we did not already know
your pain and suffering.
It has gotten bigger than life itself,
this pain, enough to swallow us all.
I know you are lost in it, and we
are close to losing our way, too.
         So,
we've thought about going on
without you, pushing past this awful place
we're all stuck in, and just moving
to higher ground, a place to rest
and consider how wrong we all have been

This, Over and Over

I am back to my day-to-day,
the routine one comes to value
as one gets older and starts to look
for sameness amid the chaos.

I am still chafing from my last
foray into the wild, unsettled
world I am privy to here.

I find myself packing identical
lunches each day, the solid,
reassuring something that I
will look fondly on at noon. I ache
for monotony, this, over and over,
the comfort of it, the distance
it puts me from surprise.

Second Baptism

We are over the crying,
no longer bewildered
by your state of affairs.
We barely blink an eye now
as we rise with your toddler
each morning, bathe and dress him,
pack his lunchbox for preschool.

Our bodies remember the rhythm
it took to raise children, the tiredness
we could push ourselves to and still
be able to load the dishwasher
and fold what was in the dryer.

He seems none the worse
for our old style of parenting,
figuring out animal puzzles
at the kitchen table while we cook,
building with Legos on the dining room floor.

There is a sort of cleansing
in it all, that second baptism. Not of fire,
just a rising up each day, certain
of what we must do.

The Space You Occupy

We cannot predict the trajectory
of your incredible fall.

If we could plot the angle,
know by the geometry of it,

where you might land, how far
from us, the degrees of separation

from your old life, we could send
a boat for you, arrange a rescue,

or pad your point of impact.
It is too fine a science, though,

a parallelogram of unknowns
that occlude the space you occupy.

Grief Shapes Us

I look at how grief shapes us,
gives us a certain way
of carrying ourselves,
      the slope
      of our shoulders,
         faces not looking forward.

This weight holds us
back from day to day living,
makes us exist on the edge
            of everything,

looking inward
for scraps of evidence
that can testify to the whys
and wherefores.

I need a reason
for missing you
from the next room over.

An Empty Place at the Table

I feel you slowly moving away
from us, leaving your boy behind,
packing your emotional bags
and checking out
of the family scene. It is so much
effort to keep us all happy, make
the days work, hold
a smile on your face and pay attention.

A quiet walk out the back door
and you're gone, no one the wiser,
least of all us. Hell, we've been staring
at an empty place at the table
for five or six months now, but we
keep setting the plate and glass out,
we place the silverware carefully,
we sit patiently and wait.

Protocols

Visiting you on the lockdown unit
was somewhat disconcerting.

I did not know the protocols
and did not follow any guidelines.

We wept in the meeting area,
let our voices rise with emotions,

and held hands across the table.
Your hair and clothes disheveled,

my heart broken, we were mostly
a matched set, outsiders forced

to toe a line we could not identify,
pray to gods we did not believe in.

His Life Goes On

You are going off to live with strangers,
hoping to get well. They know
you can no longer live alone, even
with your small boy beside you.

He stays with us now, mostly
unaware of all these changes.
His life goes on, uninterrupted,
a sippy cup, snacks, a walk

each day are what he needs.
We can give him that, and more,
while you figure out how to live
your life anchored to this planet.

A Simple Gesture

We sat down to Sunday dinner
together for the first time in months.
A simple enough gesture,
but it speaks louder than anything else
we have done lately.

You cut the meat on your son's plate,
we passed the salad, poured
the milk, we asked each other how the day
had gone, laughed at a funny thing
the young boy said.   We held
each other's gaze without wincing,
smiled and nodded so easily that you
would have thought what a nice family
we were, not witnesses to a free fall,
not people eclipsed by tragedy, we
are just sitting down to dinner together,
tonight, at least for tonight.

Put Back the Stars

Nights I slept with my cell phone,
made deals with a god I did not think
I believed in, bartered with
the universe to spare you, hold you,
mend you, put back the stars
in you that had burned out
and fallen from your sky.
                        Now there is some chance
that you are healing, mending
the cracks in your psyche,
holding on to your resolve and pulling
yourself out of the deep hole
you fell into. It is only a rumor,
a whisper of maybes, but I want
to hold onto it, grasp it tightly
and believe with every piece
of my shattered self.

The Dinosaur Game

I am guardian to the boy
who plays a dinosaur game
on the floor beside me.
He pretends with a family
of triceratops, mommy,
daddy, and three babies,
all in descending sizes,
traipsing across his unfolded
Dino-land map.

I rise
with this boy each morning,
feed him,
help him get dressed,
I buy him the dinosaurs
he configures
into the family he does not have.

Tell Her

This is a prayer, universe.
Receive it, take it up

as you would the clouds,
absorb it as you do the rain,

hold it as you do the stars,
spread out across

your velvet lap. Hold her now
as you would a child,

press her close to you
and whisper sweetly

in her ear—tell her
she must live.

All the Whys

Your collateral damage weighs
about thirty-two pounds and is
thirty-six inches tall. He asks

"why" a lot these days, not specifics,
just life in general, why
does he have to go to bed, why

does he have to take a bath, why
is his mommy not here? Everyday
sorts of questions, with ordinary answers,

except that last one, it's a killer; no one
knows quite what to say. We are all
waiting for your answer.

Growing Pain

I wait for your sobriety to take hold,
to root in you like a flower in a pot,

drive down tendrils that wrap
themselves around your heart

puling and pulling every time
you think about your life, your son,

your place in the world, enough
to make you catch your breath

with the pain of it,
the heartbreaking pain of it.

Map of My Fears

Your addiction draws lines
on my face, deep and distinct.

I look in the mirror and see
how much older I have become

because of it. I carry the weight
of my worry here, open

to the world. After I think
I have put it all inside me, it forces

its way out, platting from within
a relief map of my fears.

Wrapped Up in Normal

I wonder if it feels different
for you now, as your neurons

have calmed down, not so agitated
by the drugs, as your body

gets used to water and air again,
food, no narcotic supplements.

Do you smell different, too?
Do you recognize yourself

wrapped up in normal?
Does the lull inside your frontal lobe

feel familiar? Can you
find yourself in there?

Recovery

I am pondering the changes in you,
sitting back quietly and watching
day to day.

I know it hasn't
been easy, the walk from there
to here. There is still a pull
from within you that you fight
to overcome.

I cannot applaud just yet.
I am stuck, too, in that old way
of thinking, seeing you

from my own point of view, lost
and broken.

Out of the Maze

Your absolution comes
in bits and pieces, the cord of it
wrapped around
your self-doubt.
You cannot order up
enough forgiveness to go around,
not to soothe your boy,
or make any of us whole again.
                      You
invoke the gods of suffering,
gods of sadness, call them
to you, ask for the map
to the treasure of insight.
                      Perhaps
that will sustain you,
a thread that will lead you
out of the maze, let you kneel,
once and for all, in the light.

Metaphorically Speaking

Your father says your job is the boat
you are floating down the river on.
He says your boy is the anchor for the boat.
I say the boy is the ballast, that without him
you will float free and aimless over this river.
We are talking metaphorically:
the river is life
the boat is your salvation
your boy is your saving grace
we are the ballast that holds you to this earth.

We are, all of us, in this river dangling
our feet off the boat,
the boat that is your life,
your boy the rudder that steers it.

We are all euphemisms for love,
which flows here, unimpeded,
anchoring us all to this boat,
holding us all to the earth, as ballast does.

Back into the Fray

One hundred days did not
give you the clarity you sought,

nor did it remove any obstacles
from your path. It merely proved

to be a short respite, for all of us,
from the relentless grind

of your addiction. We laid our heads
down, collectively, and slept

a dreamless sleep, waking
to find you gone again,

back into the fray of your life,
your own war zone,

the bombs falling all around you.

Big Ironman

The one he calls Big Ironman
stands on his bedside table
each night. He guards the boy

whose mother is gone, journeying
far from home. The boy needs
this powerful one to keep him safe

until her return. He invokes
the spirit of this suited man,
asks for his power and his armor

to hold back the night, keep
his fear at bay, set the moon bright
and bring this traveler back to him.

Raising You

Raising you should be a cinch,
the knowledge in hand
having already raised my children.
Yet I've struggled at each turn,
how much should I allow,
where should the firm 'no'
be inserted?
                    I sort of forgot
how potty-training worked,
the myriad
of instructional tips and pointers
I could insert into our conversations.
                    How to present
the ABC's to a three-year old
who already had 'rehab'
in his vocabulary, and talked
about waiting for sleep to come?
                    How does one teach
the rudimentary to a child
already immersed
in extraordinary?

The Syntax of Your Texts

I got tangled in the syntax of your texts
last night, all those big words,
like guardianship and custody,

petitions, and other legal terms,
talking about the court as if it were
an entity unto itself. You threw your weight

around a bit then, through the complex
workings of a cell tower and a battery
you managed to project your attitude

all the way across town, on air,
seemingly to me. However
it was delivered, I got it. The tone,

the moxie, the social worker savvy
came through on the cell phone waves,
sent via some galaxy way beyond our own.

This Mother's Lament

I am tired of writing
about you, your addiction,
your tripped-out life.
I am tired of my sadness
leaking through these lines.
I am tired of feeling
the need to understand you,
and that feeling never
being satisfied. I am tired
of spending my hour in therapy
each week crying
about my inability to hold
the duality of who you are
in my head.

I am tired of worrying
about you, wondering
if you have a place to stay,
whether you are actively using,
or broke, saying
you are doing this
one day at a time.
I am tired of writing about you
in my head, playing out scenarios
where you die, we identify
your body and raise your son.
I am tired of the fear
that wrecks my sleep, pushes me
awake at three am and compels me
to go downstairs to my computer
and write about you.

In the Throes of Her Addiction

The hubris of you, full and dark
as you crash through this life,

unchecked and unwilling
to be anything but whatever

you want, regardless of anything
or anyone else. You as the sun,

exploding as I write this.

Paperwork

We drew up the paperwork
so you could see your boy.

We made you sign things
you didn't want to sign.

We will make you get
drug-screened, make you

give us money, make you
be supervised while you visit him,

even though you are
his mother. It has come to this,

guardianship, agreements, legal
documents, notarized pages

and the scribbled signatures
of bewildered grandparents.

You came today and saw him,
he ran into your arms as if
he remembered everything about you.

Driving Away from You

Your desperation follows me up the highway
as I drive north on vacation, seeking comfort
in old friends and new sights. Your contrition leaks
through the texts you dash off, trying
to tie me to you, to your sinking ship, to your woeful self.

       I cannot feel the sorrow anymore,
it has turned itself over to an anger that fuels
each decision I make about you.

I want lists
that will define our meetings,
protocols
for our love and kindnesses,
good manners
that will keep us with one another in a new version
of our family relationships.

       I keep asking myself
how it got to this, what wrong turn did we make
as we journeyed, so innocently, together?

Recovery Redux

So this is what it looks like:
we pass each other
in the kitchen, you
to your oatmeal, me to my eggs,
the coffee goes to both of us,
your son gets cold cereal
and juice.			His grandfather takes him
to the couch for morning cartoons.
Breakfasted, we plan the day,
you your way, us to ours,
but we'll meet up again,
come dinner time,
a group of hands to fix a meal,
hearts mending, sighs all around.

To the Universe, Clumsily

I would prostrate myself
at this moment if I could
get down on the floor quickly.
I would kneel and pray
to the universe if
my knees weren't shot.
I'd fold my body
into a yoga position and begin
to meditate if
it was possible to fold my body.

Instead I stand here bulky
and ungraceful
before you, universe
of lost souls, holder
of answers, keeper
of secrets, the one
who knows I am walking
down the wrong path
right now, hopelessly
lost in the dense woods
of guilt and regret.

Throw me a few crumbs
please, anything that might
mark my way out of this,
take me back to where
I should be, keeper
of my own self.

Clean

Halfway to your one year
anniversary we acquiesce
to your need for closeness.
We tuck you in to the bed
where you slept as a child,
in your old girlhood room.

Pull the curtains, dim
the light, we hold our breath
to see if the cure took.

Did you
Recover? Rehab? Rehash? Relive?

Can you
walk a straight line?
Piss a clean drug screen?
Wake up each day
with fresh eyes
and steady hands,
like the girl you were at 12?

We tiptoe out and draw the door closed
without a sound,
reluctant, now, to let you go.

Disparity

The day my sister is fitted
for her radiation mask
my daughter's ankle bracelet
from three months
of house arrest
is cut off. One
set free as the other
reports for her sentence:
thirty treatments, six weeks.

I inhale sharply,
breathless as this
disparity of worlds
bangs up
against my heart.

In and Out

Your son gave me a picture
he had drawn today
in art class, vivid blues
and greens, in the upper
left corner a simple "Erth",
made special with a big capital E.

He wants me
to send it to you, but I don't
know the address
for "walked away from rehab". There is no
street name for "returned to abusive boyfriend",
and no zip code
for the crack house you know downtown.

We are there all over again,
this time only a three-month respite,
a brief lull
in the din of your addiction. Your son
thinks he will be visiting you, dear daughter,
in the place where you are "getting well",
believes with all his heart you will both
go roller skating. He is planning
on holding your hand as you weave
in and out of the pulsing lights.

Recompense

You laid down the crack pipe
and took up your life again,
only looking back to count
the reasons you had lived.
Your boy beside you
each day is enough you said.
So we all walk forward
a few steps, holding
our breath to see
if this can last,
or will some terrible pull
breach the dike and drag
you back into the wash?

You say you have your own god,
one the books don't talk about,
one who is privy to your fears
and secrets. But this god
doesn't punish you, or hold you
down with guilt. And so I,
in my faithlessness, call him
to me, render my recompense,
barter for my debt.

Anything Can Happen

You emerge from this round reassured
confident that you can lick
this addiction and get your life back.

You text your plans
for the next go-round to your parents,
with thank yous and apologies in place.
You put a touch up to that episode,
black out the screwed-up part
and doll up the rest of it.

Maybe you didn't get kicked out
of the half-way house,
just asked to leave.
Maybe they'll take you back
and let you prove yourself.
Maybe you'll lay down the needle
and pick up a violin.
Who knows? Anything can happen,
anything at all.

The Gut of Your Habit

Nine months,
like giving birth to yourself,
the newness of you

the unspoiled truth of who
and what you are, nothing
to hide anymore, no secrets.

We whispered the story of your addiction,
finally telling the facts,
bare and ugly as they were,

what we'd held close in our own
secret places. We cut open
the gut of your habit,

the largesse of it, sprawling
and swollen all over our lives.
And we bled that animal,

as if it were hung on a hook
above a slaughterhouse floor.
Now only a carcass swings,

back and forth, but we are all
keeping an eye on that one, too.

Can You Spell R-E-L-A-P-S-E?

Your inability to make
a promised phone call to your son.

Your inability to show up
at his swim meet.

Your inability
to show up consistently anywhere.

I can see it
in the fresh tracks on your arms
when you get too hot and take off
your sweatshirt.

I can hear it
when the phone doesn't ring
night after night when you should be
checking in on your son.

I can feel it
when I go to bed at night, nervous
because I don't know where you are
on this earth.

More Bigger Blues

If BB King came to you
asked you to sing
the blues with him

couldn't you just wail
and never stop
wouldn't he lay that

guitar of his the one
he named Lucille down
put his arm around you

knowing your blues
are so much bigger
than his ever were?

Holding Our Breath

We walk through this
carefully
on tiptoe
over eggshells
holding our breath
so as not to wake
the sleeping beasts
snoring in their lair
lest they rise up
and drag us all down again
beneath this quaking earth.

The crack beast
the heroin beast
the alcohol beast
they walk together
upending all the furniture
in the room
as they stand up
in their
        indignancies
        offended
by the carefulness of us
the hushed ways of us
not bawling out loud
but keeping the secret
so nobody knows.

As if they can't see
your glassy eyes
your lack of a job
no car no cash no kid
who lives with you
        nothing
that we could do
to make you own this day.

On Being Thrown Out of Rehab

After one hundred and twenty days
your fear rises
to the surface of your skin
burning you like the sun.

You look for a way
to stitch up this opening
in your psyche.

The drugs themselves are secondary,
a binding to hold in
the memory of who you were.

And now
you walk among us, unseen,
the scent of you subjugated too
as if you no longer exist
anywhere.

But I remember the curve
of your ear
the whorls of hair at your neckline
the breath you took in
and released.

Suicide, By Installments

Installment one was your blackout,
back in 2005, coming home
from the bar you went down
 into a ditch off Binford Boulevard
 and came back up, skittered across
all three lanes and bounced
off the median, coming to rest
on the berm of the road,
next to the guardrail that kept you from the retention pond.

Was number two when you climbed out
 the bedroom window,
 stepped onto the sunroom roof,
 jumped down to the front porch
and went to meet your dealer on the corner,
while your son slept next to the bed you had abandoned?

The next few installments unfolded
right here, in that same city:

a room at the hotel
where paramedics
took you away
after a bad drug night,

at the Stress Center
where you were held
for the break in your psyche,

in the half-way house
where you tricked them
into giving you back
your debit card
so you could get money
to buy drugs.

I believe you completed
the sixth and seventh installments
when the EMT called to you
through the broken window
of the car that had crashed
into a concrete wall, asking you
if you could move your fingers
for him, before they tried to get you out
and load you into the ambulance.

You
shattered   cut   ruptured   bloody   sobbing
on a gurney in the ER.

How will you close the door
on this run-through
of a brand-new season?

Rewriting the Script

I dreamed I was writing poems
about you last night, you burning
in the fire of your addiction,
tied to the hopelessness of it
as if you'd already made the agreement
to ride this thing to the end,
no matter what. And then I
was frantically editing these poems,
moving your hopelessness off
the page, inserting courage
and a resilient spirit, you
saving yourself over and over.

In my dream you kept resisting
my rewrites, changing the script
back to lost and broken, the vehicle
that is your life crashed on the side
of the road, no survivors. But I
wrote you back in, crawling
from that wreckage,
a strong sponsor answering
your last cell phone call for help.
People from a nearby meeting gather
to lift you off the road,
and hold you
until the bleeding stops. In my dreams
you live, every single time.

The Words

What do you tell a daughter
on the eve of her 37th birthday?

That you love her?
                        Unquestionably
That you are grateful?
                        Yes.
That you are
inextricably entwined with her?
                        Of course.

So what new words
can be spoken on this day?

Most importantly, tell her
                you are glad that she lived,
                from a cord twisted
                around her neck
                as you tried to push her
                out into this world,
                to her days at a rehab center
                shaking off the hold
                of her addiction, and all
                the near misses between them.

Tell her you embrace it,
        that you take it into your heart.
Tell her
        that you learn the truth about love
        every time you are with her.

Acknowledgements:

"Back into the Fray"
"Rewriting the Script"
Appeared in *The Flying Island* January 2019

"Recompense"
"Back into the Fray"
"Rewriting the Script"
Grouped as a trilogy, these are part of the InVerse Hoosier Poetry Archive, under the title "Her Addiction"

"On Being Thrown Out of Rehab"
"Getting Sober"
"An Empty Place at the Table"
Published in *Last Stanza Poetry Journal Issue #2: Marginalia* (Stackfreed Press, 2020)

"Anything Can Happen"
"Recovery"
"Tell Her"
Published in *Anti-Heroin Chic* (October 2021)

"The Words"
Published by the *Tipton Poetry Journal* (December 2021)

"In and Out"
Published in *Anti-Heroin Chic* (February 2022)

"Second Baptism"
Published in *The Indianapolis Review* (November 2022)

Mary Sexson is author of the award-winning book, *103 in the Light, Selected Poems 1996-2000* (Restoration Press), and co-author of *Company of Women, New and Selected Poems* (Chatter House Press). Her poetry has appeared in *Tipton Poetry Journal, Laureate, Hoosier Lit, Flying Island, New Verse News, Grasslands Review,* and *Last Stanza Poetry Journal,* among others. She has recent work in *Reflections on Little Eagle Creek, Anti-Heroin Chic,* and *Last Stanza Poetry Journal* Issue #7. She has three Pushcart Prize nominations. Sexson's poetry is part of the INverse Poetry Archives for Hoosier Poets.

Mary Sexson's poetry has also been a part of several public projects. In 2006 her work was chosen for a public project called Shared Spaces/Shared Voices, a collaboration between the Arts Council of Indianapolis and IndyGo. Her poem "Solstice" was mounted on a placard and rode on an IndyGo bus for a year. Mary also was a part of 2 Arts Kaleidoscope projects. The first was Art & Poems (2008). This project was in collaboration with Gallery 308 in Muncie, Indiana, and the Community Foundation of Muncie and Delaware County, Inc. In 2009 Gallery 308 created The Founder's Poetry Gathering, "a celebration of the relationship between words and visual art" which Sexson was part of. Sexson was also involved in the River Writings Project, where her poem "Oh, Sycamore!" was mounted as a sign, in the Prophetstown State Park, alongside a walking trail, and then at Falls of the Ohio State Park. In 2020 and 2021 the Indiana Writers Center collaborated with Spirit and Place to bring poets together, first for their pandemic writing, with an online publication, *What Was and Will Be.* Sexson's poem, "Close" was chosen to be choreographed by Dance Kaleidoscope as part of the Spirit and Place presentations. In 2021 Indiana Writers Center created a project, Leave Them Something, for writers to reflect on a collection of artworks by Edith Vonnegut regarding pollution and climate change. Sexson's poem "Angel, Bound in Plastic," was chosen by Dance Kaleidoscope to be choreographed. One of Sexson's poems was recently chosen to be included in one of the three Polaris anthologies going to the Moon! This project came about as part of The Lunar Codex Project. More than 67,000 works of contemporary creative artists from all over the world will be attached to the various rockets' landers, and end up on the Moon's southern pole. The anthologies will be published here in February 2023, and this digital anthology leaves from NASA, to the Moon, in 2024. Her work is part of the INverse Poetry Archives for Hoosier Poets.

masexson.wordpress.com   facebook.com/poetrysisters

www.ingramcontent.com/pod-product-compliance
Lightning Source LLC
Chambersburg PA
CBHW031126160426
43192CB00008B/1131